Map & Guide
to Exploring the

Land's End Peninsula

&

The Tinners Way
—— Including ——

St Michael's Mount
Penzance   St Ives
Mousehole Lamorna
Land's End St Just
&
The Complete
Peninsula Coast Path

GW00602652

Friendly Guide
• *First Edition* •

Safety by the Sea

Many fatalities occur because people ignore simple and common sense rules when they are by the sea. NEVER take the sea for granted.

Do not swim after a meal or after consuming alcohol.

Never swim off headlands - strong currents can pull you out to sea even on a calm day.

Do not let children go into the sea on an airbed or inflatable - they can quickly be drawn out to sea by offshore winds or on a riptide.

Never touch strange objects washed up by the sea - dangerous canisters containing flares, munitions and chemicals are sometimes brought ashore. If you find something suspicious inform the Coastguard or Police.

ALWAYS obey lifeguards - they are aware of dangers that may not be apparent to you.

Never approach the edge of a cliff - it may be unstable or slippery.

If you are exploring a cliff base be aware of the tide and unstable cliffs above you.

Do not sit or walk close to rocks that are being swept by waves - an unexpectedly large wave can pull you into the sea.

Be aware of other people who may be in danger. If in doubt, telephone 999 and ask for the Coastguard - you may save a life.

Warning flags at the beach

 Bathing safe between flags

 No swimming - area between flags reserved for surfing, canoeing and other water sports.

 No swimming - hazardous conditions

Published by Cormorant Design
PENZANCE
Cornwall
Telephone (01736) 369194
© Neil Reid 1998
ISBN 0 9520874 9 9

Picture Credits:

Page 8 - RCHME, © Crown Copyright. Pages 5, 7, 9, 28 - © Cornwall Archaeological Unit/Cornwall County Council. Pages 16/17, 33, 37, 41, 45 - The Royal Institution of Cornwall. Page 34 - The National Trust. Pages 6, 10, 15, 18, 23, 26, 30, 46 & 47 & back cover - Paul Watts. Front cover & pages 19, 35, 42, 43 - Andrew Besley. Page 25 - Frank Gibson.

The Publishers would like to gratefully acknowledge the help and assistance provided by the Cornwall Archaeological Unit, The National Trust and the Royal Institution of Cornwall in the preparation of this guidebook.

The maps in this book are based on the Ordnance Survey 1909 1:10,560 series maps. The depiction of a footpath or track in this guidebook is not evidence of a right of way.

The plans of Carn Euny prehistoric village and fogou are based on the work of Patricia Christie, who excavated the site, and are used with the kind permission of Mr D Christie.

Contents

Introduction

It has become a cliche to describe West Cornwall as a mysterious place - a place where nothing is quite what it seems. Yet behind that cliche there is an essential truth because just under the surface of the modern landscape are the surprising complete remnants of a prehistoric landscape. There are very few places in Britain where you feel closer to our prehistoric ancestors than in the Land's End Peninsula. Many of the existing field boundaries are 2,000 years old and the Stone Age tombs or *quoits* that dot the hills on the north coast are as old as the pyramids in Egypt. The moors and hills are decorated with monuments and tombs, enigmatic stone circles, standing stones and whole prehistoric villages. The people that live here today also belong to that continuum so that ancient Christian sites such as Madron Well are still dressed with rags in an echo of a pagan era.

The Land's End Peninsula is shaped like a wedge, with a crescent of exposed hills and moorland on the north and west coasts. The more sheltered, low lying agricultural land and the safe anchorage of **Mount's Bay** lie to the south and east. One of the best ways to start exploring the area is to get your bearings from higher ground in the north. **Trencrom Hill**, **Sancreed Beacon**, **Chapel Carn Brea** and **Carn Galva** are all easily accessible. The drainage of the area is radial, but the bias of high ground to the north means the northward flowing streams sometimes have to flow less than a mile to reach the sea. Even these small streams feel verdant and luxurious when contrasted with the salt bitten and exposed moorland that surrounds them (See: walk 4 Wicca & River Cove). The southerly streams by contrast, cut the deep green wooded valleys of **Lamorna**, **Penberth** and **St Loy** (See: Walk 1.)

Few areas of the moors are truly wild, but they do support a rich wildlife including kestrels and other birds of prey. The sea has a tremendous influence on the flora and fauna. Only a few specialised plants can survive on the exposed coast. They have adapted to be able to resist the burning effect of the salt sea spray from the violent autumn and winter storms. Prostrate heathers cling to the ground and trees only survive in the sheltered valleys on the south of the Peninsula. The sea has a moderating effect on the climate bringing cooling sea breezes in the summer and warming the cold air in the winter so that palm trees flourish in sheltered areas. Azaleas and camellias thrive in the garden at **Trengwainton** and even on the lee of **St Michael's Mount**.

Pods of dolphins and whales are often spotted from the cliffs and sometimes the dolphins can be seen surfing the breaking waves at Sennen Cove or riding the bow wave of the *Scillonian III*. The double fins of huge but harmless basking sharks are often seen as they trawl the inshore waters for krill and plankton and grey seals breed in the deep and secluded sea caves around **Land's End** and **Nanjizal Bay**. **St Ives Island** and **Gwennap Head** are the best places to observe migrant birds such as puffins. The *Scillonian III* makes special trips in the autumn to the area off Land's End for watching sea birds and pleasure boats leave Penzance Harbour to follow the coastline to **Porthcurno** and **Lamorna**.

The geology of the underlying rocks have shaped the history of this part of Cornwall. The Land's End Peninsula is a large dome shaped island of granite implanted about 300 million years as a molten mass into older surrounding sedimentary rocks. These overlying rocks have been worn away over many millions of years exposing the granite and now they only form a fringe around the coast of the peninsula. This is especially clear on the north coast where they form a shelf between the moors and the coast which is in places only a few fields wide. It can be spectacularly viewed from

The Bronze Age stone circle at Boscawen-un which may be as much as 5,000 years old. This is the most atmospheric of the Land's End stone circles and lies close to the later Iron Age village at Carn Euny. This area is very rich in prehistoric remains - see pages 28 to 31.

Carn Galva & **Zennor Hill** (See: parts 8 & 9). The Land's End granite boss is believed to be connected deep underground to other nearby granite areas. To the west, and visible from **Gwennap Head** and **Land's End**, lie the Isles of Scilly; to the east is the Carnmenellis boss that forms the high ground between Redruth and Falmouth. Smaller outcrops of granite occur between these larger areas notably at **St Michael's Mount**.

A strong characteristic of soils that overlie a granite bedrock are the large boulders or *moorstone* that sit above the surface even in cultivated fields. The moorstone has to be cleared to enable the land to be cultivated and because of this, it is assumed that at least some of the field boundaries probably date from the Neolithic period (4000-2500BC) when agriculture was first practised here. Also characteristic are the rocky crags or *carns* whose huge cubic boulders appear to have been precariously stacked one on another, as if by a giant. The cubic system of joints was formed deep underground as the molten granite slowly cooled, shrunk and fractured. Once the granite is exposed, the natural weathering process erodes the rock along these lines of weakness until sometimes huge blocks weighing many tons will rest on a tiny point of contact with the block below. These stones can then sometimes be rocked backwards and forwards and are called *logan stones*. The most famous is the **Logan Rock** near **Treen** on the south coast which unfortunately no longer rocks having been dislodged as a bet in the 19th century. A smaller example is the logan stone at **Bosigran** just inside Bosigran Iron Age cliff castle. Another feature of these carns are the cup shaped basins that form naturally on the highest stones. It was once thought these were cut by druids to catch the blood of sacrificial victims. The carns often take on anthropomorphic shapes and many are named after animals such as **The Horseback** near **Zennor** and the **Gurnard's Head** near **Treen** on the north coast. This adds to the feeling that the landscape itself is alive especially when the frequent sea mists swirl around the carns.

The granite of the Land's End Peninsular has given up two vital components that have shaped the lives of the people that live here. Firstly, it contains the mineral veins or *lodes* of tin and copper that have been mined in some form for the last 3,000 years and secondly, it provides a durable stone for quarrying and building. In fact it is so durable that some prehistoric houses are still clearly visible after 3,000 years and many of the field boundaries on the high ground are probably of a similar age.

The Land's End Peninsula is very rich in archeological sites and what makes it particularly special is that so much of the accompanying prehistoric landscape has survived too. Nowhere in Britain are you more acutely aware of the presence of prehistoric man, almost as if you turned suddenly you might catch a glimpse of

Lanyon Quoit

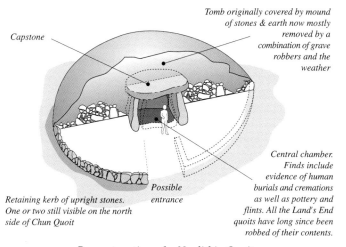

Tomb originally covered by mound of stones & earth now mostly removed by a combination of grave robbers and the weather

Capstone

Central chamber. Finds include evidence of human burials and cremations as well as pottery and flints. All the Land's End quoits have long since been robbed of their contents.

Possible entrance

Retaining kerb of upright stones. One or two still visible on the north side of Chun Quoit

Reconstruction of a Neolithic Quoit.
Best examples-Lanyon Quoit, Chun Quoit, Zennor Quoit & Mulfra Quoit

one of them out of the corner of your eye. The historic predominance of pastoral agriculture has left whole areas undisturbed by the plough for 5,000 years. Coupled with the inherent durability of granite structures this has left a tapestry of prehistoric settlements, field boundaries, fortifications and sacred sites.

The earliest known inhabitants of West Cornwall were the hunter gathers of the Old Stone Age. As far as we know they probably lived a nomadic life gathering berries and plants and following herds of wild animals on which their food supply depended. The only artifacts we have are their sharp flint arrowheads and stone axes, some of which are on show at the **Penlee House Museum** in Penzance. About 6,000 years ago a new group of people slowly moved into West Cornwall these were the Neolithic or New Stone Age peoples. They probably crossed into Britain from Europe via a land bridge sometime after the last ice age 10,000 years ago, when sea levels were much lower. The Neolithic communities seem to have become less nomadic perhaps cultivating crops and domesticating some animals and moving on to new sites when the soil became exhausted.

There is no conclusive evidence of Neolithic settlements in West Cornwall although it is possible that **Trencrom Hill** and **Carn Galva** may have been Neolithic sites. They have remains of massive walls and follow a characteristic Neolithic pattern of linking together natural rock outcrops. The nearest proven Neolithic structure is at Carn Brea near Redruth clearly visible 15 miles to the east from **Trencrom Hill**.

It is the Neolithic people who built the first monuments in West Cornwall. These are the Penwith chamber tombs known locally

Part of a prehistoric pattern of tiny fields at Bosigran below Carn Galva. At the centre of the photograph is a courtyard house settlement. This dates the field boundaries to at least to the Iron Age 1,500 to 2,000 years ago.

as *quoits* which were constructed about 5,000 years ago. A number of fine examples of these burial tombs stand on the chain of hills above the north coast and are on the route of an ancient track called the **Tinners Way** (see page 32). A second, later wave of Neolithic settlers built the Scillonian chamber tombs or *entrance graves* that are particular to West Cornwall and the Isles of Scilly. The best example being **Tregiffian Barrow** near **Lamorna** (see page 20).

At sometime about 4,000 years ago, a new wave of settlers slowly moved into the Land's End Peninsula. These were the Bronze Age peoples. They brought with them a knowledge of metal working and started to mine the copper veins in the cliffs and the tin deposits in the stream beds to make tools and weapons. It was the Bronze Age people that constructed the stone circles and standing stones or *menhirs*.

There are numerous theories concerning the role of stone circles - they obviously had some ritualistic or religious symbolism but unfortunately we will probably never know what function they originally served. Indeed they have probably taken on many totally unrelated functions throughout history, just as any building today might be adapted for a new use. The stone circles are still in use today and sometimes when you are driving late at night past one of these circles you can see ghostly naked figures dancing around in the moonlight. However it is just as likely to be a Young Farmers' drunken social night as the local witches coven. The best and most atmospheric stone circle is at **Boscawen-ûn**, just off the A30 between Drift and Crows-an-wra. The best time to visit is very early in the morning or at sun set.

The Bronze Age people also constructed burial mounds similar to the Scillonian chamber tombs of the Neolithic period, a good example being **Mayon Barrow** near **Sennen Cove**. They lived in settlements of *hut circles* or *round houses* the remains of which are very common throughout this area. An exceptionally well preserved example is **Bodrifty Prehistoric Village** near Mulfra Hill (see page 39).

About 2,500 years ago the Iron Age people we call the Celts pushed west into Cornwall. They developed a new form of house that incorporated the round house but added small stores, workrooms and accommodation for animals around an unroofed courtyard. Despite the apparent sophistication of this house plan with its semiprivate spaces, the popularity of the *courtyard house* never spread outside of West Cornwall. The excavated Iron Age villages at **Chysauster** and **Carn Euny** are of national importance. What makes them special is the way one can glimpse something of the ordinary life of our ancestors.

Chysauster Prehistoric Village. Classic examples of Iron Age Courtyard Houses. Top right is the semidetached house. A trackway runs between the two rows of houses. Houses 4 & 6 on the lower row are the best preserved examples only missing their roofs.

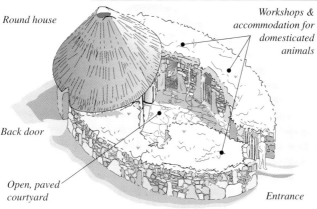

Round house

Workshops & accommodation for domesticated animals

Back door

Open, paved courtyard

Entrance

Reconstruction of an Iron Age Courtyard House
Best examples-Chysauster, Carn Euny & Porthmeor.

I particularly like House 3. It must be the first example of a semidetached house in Britain, predating Hampstead Garden Suburb by at least 1,500 years.

A peculiar structure associated with Iron Age villages are the underground passages or *fogous*. We have no clear idea as to their function, but they may have been used as a cold stores for food or, it has been suggested that they may have been places of refuge for when the village was under attack. The best example is the fogou at **Carn Euny** (see part 5). The Iron Age was a time of war and strife and almost every good defensive site was reinforced with earth ramparts during this time. The best hill forts are **Caer Bran** (see part 5) and **Chun Castle** (see part 8). The best cliff castles are **Treryn Dinas** (see walk 2) and **Maen Castle** (see part 4). Most of the Iron Age sites were peacefully abandoned in the centuries after AD500 when the present pattern of tiny hamlets started to develop.

From the 6th century onwards a wave of Celtic Christian missionaries arrived in Cornwall from Wales and Ireland. The Romans had brought Christianity to Britain but in many places it died away as Roman influence faded after they left Britain in AD410. What survived in Wales and Ireland was a monastic and hermitical religion. These men and women became the *Cornish saints* and they found a ready acceptance in these wild western lands. The early saints arrived by sea and set up sacred enclosures where they landed. As a result we have the coves of St Sennen, St Loy and St Leven, St Clement's Isle at Mousehole and numerous other isolated churches and holy wells. They built small rectangular chapels many on the cliffs such as at **St Levan** near **Porthcurno**. The best preserved is **Madron Chapel** and **Holy Well**. Perhaps the first monuments in the sacred enclosure would have been the Celtic crosses that are so reminiscent of the Bronze Age menhirs. There are hundreds of crosses

The ruined stone ramparts of Chun Castle Iron Age hillfort. The best example of its kind on the Land's End Peninsula. Just below the castle lies Chun Quoit and a number of other archaeological sites including the ruined Iron Age village of Bosullow Trehyllys

throughout Cornwall many carved with Christ figures. The best in this area are in **Sancreed Churchyard** (see part 5). The Celtic church took on some of the aspects of Celtic religion and to this day many holy wells are still decorated with coloured rags.

Since the later medieval period the economy has been sustained by fishing, agriculture and mining. Often miners also had to be farmers and fishermen in order to scrape a living together. There is a brief of history of mining on pages 36 & 37. The coming of the railway at the end of the 19th century opened new markets in the big cities. Daffodils were grown in tiny fields on the sheltered cliffs around **Lamorna** and **Mousehole** and market gardening flourished around Penzance. The railway also brought visitors to the Land's End Peninsula and as the traditional industries have struggled or declined tourism has become more important.

Despite setbacks fishing still thrives at Newlyn. The port lands the highest value catch in the UK. Many of the more exotic fish and much of the shell fish leave the port for the London markets and by lorry via the Plymouth-Roscoff ferry for the Continent. Small boats from **Penberth**, **Cape Cornwall**, **Treen** and **St Ives** work the reefs for lobsters and crabs. Pilchard fishing was once an established industry in the 19th century and continues at **The Pilchard Works** in **Newlyn**, the last working factory of its type in Cornwall.

Geevor Mine was the last tin mine in West Cornwall when it closed in 1992. This finally ended a continuous 3,000 year history of mining. It is impossible overestimate the symbolic importance of the death of the mining industry to Cornish people. It may in part be due to the dark Celtic imagination. There must be some connection between the dark moorland springs and holy wells that were thought to be the entrance to the underworld, and the gaping chasms and shafts that punctuated the mining landscape. Many of the mining sites have been deserted for over 100 years and are now being absorbed back into the land. Spoil heaps contaminated with arsenic and heavy metals are being recolonised and now provide rare habitats. The hundreds of open shafts support colonies of bats - a species under threat in the rest of the country. The wild West Cornwall landscape has always been in a state of change and it has always inspired the imagination. That is as much true today as it was 5,000 years ago when the quoits were first being built by our ancestors.

Further Reading:

Belerion-Ancient sites of Land's End - Craig Weatherhill. *An excellent introduction to the ancient landscape. Outlines the history and has a detailed gazetteer of sites.*

St Michael's Mount - Cornwall Archeological Unit/Pete Herring. *Detailed account of the history of the mount.*

The National Trust publish two booklets of the area

No.10 West Penwith: St Ives to Pendeen and No.11 West Penwith Cape Cornwall to Penberth

A Quick Guide on what to do & How to do it

Porthcurno with Pedn Vounder Beach and The Logan Rock

Information

St Ives TIC. The Guildhall. Telephone: (01736) 796297

Penzance TIC. The bus/train station. Telephone: (01736) 362207

Banks

Penzance & St Ives have all the major high street banks. St Just has part time branches of Barclays and Lloyds Banks. Newlyn has a part time branch of Barclays. They are generally open in the morning but none have cash machines. *Cashback* is available from supermarkets and Coop stores.

Hospitals

The West Cornwall Hospital in Penzance has casualty facilities although as we go to press they are under threat of downgrading or closure. Ring 999 if you require any emergency service including the coastguard.

Buses & Trains

From Penzance there are regular buses to Land's End, St Ives, St Just & Pendeen and half hourly services to Newlyn & Mousehole. There is a summer service to Lamorna. From St Ives bus service 15 follows the scenic north coast road to Land's End. The train service between Penzance & St Ives follows the Hayle estuary and coast with wonderful views over St Ives Bay.

Best Places to Picnic

Trencrom Hill

Take a picnic to this Iron Age Hill fort. Great views in all directions. Good place to bring children. Turn off the B3311 at Cripplesease. Tiny National Trust car park.

Zennor Head

Picnic in the evening on top of one the carns that look out over the sea towards the setting sun. Not for those afraid of heights or with small children. Finish the evening off in the Tinner's Arms at Zennor.

Best Beach Guide

Many of the beaches in West Cornwall all but disappear at high water so be sure to check tide times before you set off. You can buy tide timetables in most newsagents or check times in the local newspaper, *The Cornishman*. The popular family beaches at Marazion, Porthcurno, Sennen, St Ives and Porthkidney have lifeguards during the season. Dogs are banned from most beaches between Easter and 1st October - the exceptions are marked 🐕 .

🐕 Marazion Beach & Long Rock

Good sheltered family beaches. Marazion has fine golden sand, children's adventure playground and all facilities. Long Rock is a more pebbly beach but usually more quiet than Marazion. Wind sail tuition & water ski hire at Marazion.

🐕 Pedn Vounder

Sublime beach - one of the best beaches in Cornwall. Descent from

the cliff is steep and difficult but worth the reward. The beach
disappears at high water so check tide times before going. Pedn is
an unofficial naturist beach. Nearest facilities at Porthcurno.

Porthcurno
Extremely popular beach with fine golden sand even at high water.
Car Parking, toilets and cafes during the season. Tours of the cliff
tunnels and war communications centre leave from the hut by the
beach. The Minack theatre sits on the cliffs west of the cove.

Porth Chapel
Small steeply shelving beach reached by difficult path over rocks.
No facilities. Park by church. Usually less crowded than Porthcurno.

Porthgwarra
Tiny sheltered beach in the lee of Gwennap Head. Car park, toilets
and ice cream shop. The beach losses the sun in late afternoon.

Sennen Cove
Majestic expanse of golden sand and the favourite beach of many
in West Cornwall. Exposed to Atlantic swell means that swimming
can sometimes be hazardous. Beach is manned by lifeguards. Shops,
pub at Sennen Cove.

Gwynver Beach
Much used by surfers and likely to be less crowded than neighbouring
Sennen. There is a long but straightforward descent to beach from
the car park on Trevedra cliff - come early as it can fill up quickly.
No facilities.

Portheras Cove
One of the few beaches on the north coast. Rarely busy. Razor sharp
pieces of metal from an old wreck mean it is advisable to wear shoes
at all times. Park at Pendeen Lighthouse or Chypraze and 10 minute
walk. No facilities. Teas at Manor Farm.

Porthmeor Beach - St Ives
Glorious sandy beach beneath the Tate Gallery. Very popular in the
summer especially with surfers. Cafe and loos. Park above the Tate
Gallery.

Porthminster Beach & Carbis Bay
Both beaches accessible from stations on the Penzance - St Ives
railway line. All facilities.

Places to Visit

St Michael's Mount
Romantic castle perched on large granite outcrop in Mount's Bay.
Linked to the mainland by a causeway covered at high water.
Ferryboats transport visitors when the causeway is covered. The
castle & gardens are not open every day so check before you go.
National Trust cafe, shop and toilets on the Mount.

Penlee House Gallery & Museum
Recently extended and refurbished museum. Has a collection of
local archaeological finds from Stone Age artifacts to Victorian
objects. Houses a collection of paintings from the Newlyn School
of Artists that worked here at the end of the last century. Set in the
grounds of Penlee Park with good cafe - I recommend the Italian
chocolate cake. Children's playground nearby.

Golowan Festival & Mazey Day
Two week festival of music, theatre, dance leading up to the
midsummer solstice at the end of June. The festival culminates in
Mazey Day on the nearest Saturday to midsummer.

Trengwainton Garden
National Trust garden and home of the Bolitho Family whose success
as bankers and tin mine owners financed the building of the house
and garden. The garden has a wonderful display of azaleas in the

spring. The house is not open to the public.

Royal Cornwall Geological Museum

Next to St John's Hall in the centre of Penzance. Mineral collection built up from specimens discovered in local mines plus dinosaur footprints.

West Cornwall Maritime Festival

Held every 2 years. In 1998 between 10-14th July. A celebration of the sea that involves races, fairs, music and exhibitions. For more information - Tel: 01736 362341.

Boat Trips

Leave from Penzance Harbour to view the coast to St Michael's Mount & Lamorna. Fishing trips also available.

Isles of Scilly

Day trips to the Isles of Scilly leave from the Heliport at Penzance. The flight takes about 25 minutes. The helicopter will take you straight to the island of Tresco with its world renowned tropical gardens at Tresco Abbey.

National Lighthouse Museum

A museum to the men and the equipment of the lighthouse service. Housed in the Trinity House Depot at Penzance Harbour.

Mousehole Wild Bird Hospital

Founded by two sisters in the 1930's the hospital cares for injured birds. Open to the public.

Museum of Submarine Telegraphy

Many of this country's undersea communications cables come ashore at Porthcurno Beach. The museum is housed in tunnels and bunkers dug into the granite cliffs by tin miners in World War II in order to protect this strategically important site.

Land's End Theme Park

Attractions include a full size lifeboat, pet corner and exhibitions on the sea birds that pass Land's End during migration. Can be very crowded on overcast days. Magnificent setting.

Levant Engine House

Perched on the edge of a cliff this is the only working, steam driven, pumping engine left in Cornwall. Adjacent to Geevor Mine.

Geevor Tin Mine Museum

Geevor was the last working tin mine in West Cornwall when it closed in 1993. There are tours of the surface and underground workings - a must for those interested in the mining history of the area. Shop, cafe and information.

Wayside Museum at Zennor

Small and intimate award winning museum, illustrating the life of local working people in the last century.

Tate of the West

Permanent collection of Cornish artists' work from St Ives and the Land's End Peninsula. Coffee shop on the top floor overlooking Porthmeor Beach. May be very crowded at peak times.

Barbara Hepworth Museum

Celebrated sculptor who lived and worked in this studio and garden for 30 years. Run by the Tate Gallery. A ticket to the main gallery at Porthmeor allows you free entry here.

Total Eclipse of the Sun

On Wednesday 11th August 1999 at 11.10am there will be a total eclipse of the sun on the Land's End Peninsula.

Local Feasts

Most villages have a feast day or even a week long festival to celebrate their local saint. Ask at the TIC for more details.

1. Marazion, Penzance & Newlyn

Between them Marazion, Penzance and Newlyn account for almost two thirds of the population of the Land's End Peninsular. They perch on the rim of the sheltered basin of Mount's Bay - the only safe anchorage for many miles on this unforgiving coastline. Ocean going tugs are often posted in the bay ready to rush to the aid of any ship in trouble in the Western Approaches and the Penlee Lifeboat stationed in Newlyn Harbour has a long and proud history of life-saving. In the middle of the bay stands the romantic castle of **St Michael's Mount** which dominates views from all directions.

St Michael's Mount

Tin was traded from here in Roman times and probably for hundreds of years before that. A monastery was established in the 12th century attached to Mont St Michel in Normandy. Its strategic importance led Henry VIII to make it a fortress after the Dissolution of the Monasteries in 1535. In this role it was one of the last outposts of the royalist cause during the English Civil War and eventually fell to the Parliamentarian Army in 1646. Sir John Aubyn was an officer in the this army and he became so enchanted with the Mount that he brought it from the Crown. His family still live here.

Marazion

Marazion was a thriving market town in the 10th century when Penzance was just a hovel of fisherman's huts. Its prosperity was due the large numbers of pilgrims that came to worship at the Benedictine Monastery on St Michael's Mount. It was also a point of departure for the important medieval pilgrimage route to Santiago De Compostela in Spain. Even today the medieval harbour below St Michael's Mount is one of the largest in Cornwall although now the only traffic are the ferry boats taking visitors to and from the Mount when the causeway is covered.

Penzance

Penzance is very much a working town serving the large agricultural and rural hinterland of West Cornwall. A small early Christian chapel once stood on the Battery rocks and the present church stands proudly above the harbour like a beacon - *Pen zance* is Cornish for *holy headland*. The original fishing village was based around the present day harbour. As Penzance grew in importance, partly as a result of its status as a Stannary town - where tin was assayed and traded, the commercial centre of the town moved towards the Green Market and Market Jew Street. The two areas are linked by **Chapel Street** with its pubs, restaurants and nightclubs.

Penzance harbour and its wet dock (the harbour gate is shut as the tide falls to keep ships within the dock afloat at low water) are always busy. Small coasters and trawlers use the dry dock as do many tenders from the naval dockyard at Devonport. The dock is used by increasing numbers of yachts in the summer. There are few better ways to finish an evening than with a stroll around the harbour or along the Promenade.

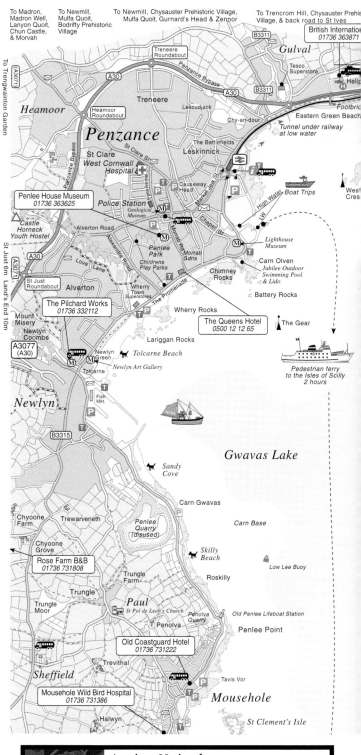

A unique National Award Winning factory showing the fascinating history of pilchard fishing in Cornwall

Open from

10.00 to 6.00 Mon to Fri

10.00 - 4.00 Saturdays

4th April - 30th November

Up from Newlyn Bridge next to the Meadery

Newlyn, Penzance, Cornwall   Tel 01736 332112

THE Pilchard Works

HERITAGE MUSEUM

NEWLYN CORNWALL

Sole producers and exporters of traditional Cornish salted pilchards

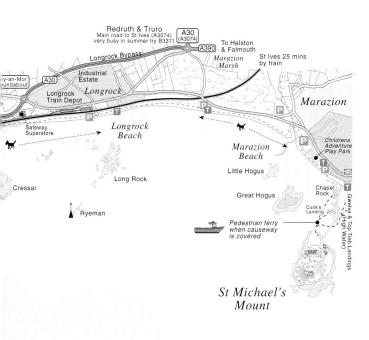

Redruth & Truro
Main road to St Ives (A3074) very busy in summer try B3311

A30 (A3074)

A390

To Helston & Falmouth

St Ives 25 mins by train

Longrock Bypass

Marazion Marsh

Industrial Estate

A30

Longrock Train Depot

Longrock

y-an-Mor undabout

Safeway Superstore

Longrock Beach

Marazion

Childrens Adventure Play Park

Marazion Beach

Little Hogus

Long Rock

Cressar

Great Hogus

Chapel Rock

Cook's Landing

Gwelva & Top Treb Landings (High Water)

Ryeman

Pedestrian ferry when causeway is covered

St Michael's Mount

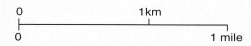

0   1km

0   1 mile

Mazey day in Penzance.
In recent years interest in reinstating and retaining old traditions has led to the expansion of the Feast of St John into the two week Golowan Festival climaxing in Mazey Day. Local school children parade though Penzance carrying sculptures and constructions of all manner of things - from pagan greenmen to bumble bees. On the eve of Mazey Day much dancing and making merry ends in the election of the mock mayor and fireworks at the Jubilee swimming pool after the pubs shut.

Please mention this Friendly Guide when replying to advertisements

Hauling in a catch of pilchards

Newlyn

The fishing industry has taken a few knocks in recent years but Newlyn still has the most valuable landings of any port in the country. The fish market starts about 7am and you can find almost every type of fish on sale from huge sun fish to tiny sprats. In recent years some boats have travelled further afield to catch tuna. Even today with all our technology it is still a dangerous and hazardous industry and there is not a year that passes without the loss of fishermen at sea. Mount Misery above Newlyn was where the fish wives used to gather, anxiously awaiting the return of sons, brothers and husbands from their voyages out to sea.

Newlyn Gallery was set up to exhibit the work of the *Newlyn Society of Artists* who established a colony here in the late 19th century and who left a wonderful record of the fishing industry and the people that worked in it. Many of their works can been seen at **Penlee House Gallery** in Penzance. The Newlyn Gallery now tends to concentrate on more contemporary work.

If you have time its worth wandering around some of the small alleys with their lovely old houses decorated with red and pink geraniums in the summer. The surprisingly large number of pubs in Newlyn cater for the fishermen who spend up to two weeks at sea. As payment they get a proportion of the sale value of the catch, part of which usually gets spent in the pub.

Penlee Point

The old Lifeboat Station on Penlee Point used to house the Penlee Lifeboat *Solomon Browne*. She was lost with all hands just before Christmas in 1981 whilst attempting to rescue the crew of the *Union Star*, wrecked below Boscawen Point to the west side of Mousehole. The replacement boat is now permanently berthed at Newlyn Harbour where it is available at times when rough easterly seas prevented launching from the Penlee Point Station.

2. Mousehole, Lamorna & St Loy

This area of the Land's End Peninsula is one of the few parts of coastline sheltered from the prevailing south westerly winds. The cliffs from **Mousehole** to **Merthen Point** are covered in tiny fields once used to grow early daffodils for the London market. The sheltered aspect and the warming effect of the sea on winter temperatures creates a very mild frost-free climate allowing daffodils to flower in January and February. Today, most early blooms are forced in heated glasshouses and the fields have been left to run wild. The only clue to their past being the many varieties of flowers that have become naturalised on the cliffs. The walk between **Mousehole** and **Lamorna** along the cliffs and back via **Kemyel** is a favourite of many locals.

The area around the **Merry Maidens** stone circle has an unusually concentrated number of archaeological monuments including **Tregiffian Barrow**, a Stone Age entrance grave and the **Pipers of Boleigh**, Bronze Age menhirs. Both are exceptional examples of their kind.

Mousehole

Mousehole is the quintessential Cornish fishing village. The houses crowd around its harbour. The village has been saved from prettification by the fact that many families still live here. People travel from all over the world to see the famous display of Christmas lights around the harbour. The village was famously sacked and destroyed by the remnants of the Spanish Armada.

Lamorna Cove

The quay at Lamorna Cove was built to handle granite from the quarries on either side of the cove. The disused quarries on the eastern side of the cove are exceptionally beautiful in spring when they become secret wooded glades and the whole hillside becomes are laden with May blossom.

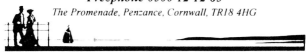
Please mention this Friendly Guide when replying to advertisements

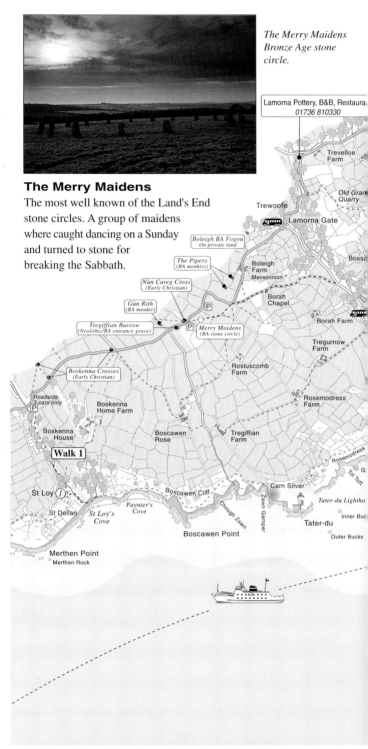

*The Merry Maidens
Bronze Age stone
circle.*

Lamorna Pottery, B&B, Restaura
01736 810330

The Merry Maidens

The most well known of the Land's End
stone circles. A group of maidens
where caught dancing on a Sunday
and turned to stone for
breaking the Sabbath.

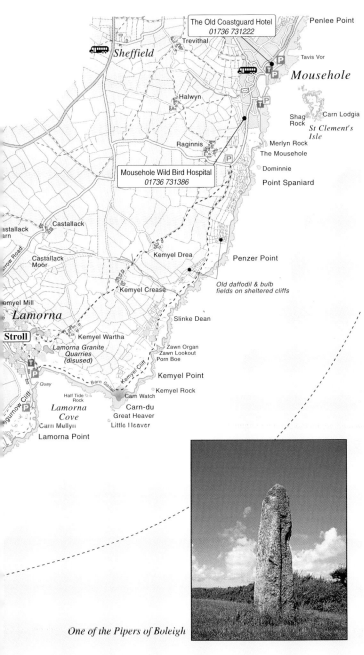

One of the Pipers of Boleigh

The Pipers of Boleigh

The Pipers are a pair of huge, enigmatic bronze age menhirs - the largest in Cornwall. They align with, but are not visible from the edge of the Merry Maidens stone circle and are therefore probably related in some way to use of the circle. The pipers were playing the tune for the Merry Maidens dance before they too were turned to stone.

Please mention this Friendly Guide when replying to advertisements

Tregiffian Barrow

Just by the side of the road west of the Merry Maidens lies this late Stone Age entrance grave - it is at least 4,000 years old. The retaining kerb is still clearly visible. Inside the chamber is a carved, pitted stone similar to naturally eroded stones on the top of carns. Folklore often associates this sort of stone with druids, who where supposed to have use them to catch blood from sacrifices. The floor of the tomb has yielded the remains of human cremations.

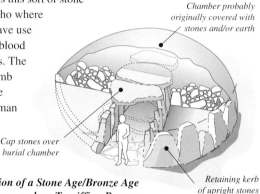

Chamber probably originally covered with stones and/or earth

Cap stones over burial chamber

Retaining kerb of upright stones

Reconstruction of a Stone Age/Bronze Age Entrance Grave such as Tregiffian Barrow

Gûn Rith Menhir

Bronze Age menhir in a field boundary just over the road from Tregiffian Barrow. As with the Pipers this seems to be specifically related to the function of the Merry Maidens - whatever that was.

Walk 1. Woodland Walk to St Loy's Cove

This walk is at its best in May when bluebells cover the floor of the wood. There are lots of fallen trees that children will love to climb on. St Loy's Cove is exposed - the waves are spectacular on a stormy day. There is no beach and bathing would be dangerous here.

Distance: 1¹/₂ miles round trip - 2 hours.

Going: Generally OK - steep climb down to the valley bottom from the coast path on the Merthen Point side of the Cove. As an alternative you might just continue on the coast path around to Merthen Point.

Car Parking: Limited roadside parking for 3 cars just before the small bridge at the head of St Loy Valley. If there is no room there, it is possible to park on the road verge near the Boskenna Crosses and walk down the hill but do not park in front of farm gates.

Pub/Refreshments : Cafe/restaurant at Lamorna Pottery. Nearest pubs are the Lamorna Wink in Lamorna Valley or the Logan Rock at Treen (see next section).

Follow the path through the woods. At the bottom of the valley cross the stream and continue as the path rises and follows the side of the valley. You will come to a wooden stile on your left with a sign showing it to be the coast path. Cross the stile. This path descends very steeply to St Loy's Cove.

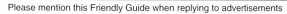

3. Logan Rock, Porthcurno & Gwennap Head

Now we start to move away from the sheltered cliffs and wooded valleys towards the exposed western coast. The raging gales bring in waves with a fetch of hundreds of miles. Even on a calm day in summer the underlying swell maybe a metre high and can bring in powerful freak waves. During gales the crashing waves can bring spray inland for many miles - pruning the exposed sides of the few trees so that they become lopsided. The sheltered buds grow on normally so that the trees look as if they are being permanently blown by a gale.

Penberth

Penberth Cove still has a number of boats fishing from the slip mostly for crab and lobster but also for mackerel.

Treryn Dinas & the Logan Rock

See next page.

Porthcurno

Beautiful beach and the land terminal of numerous undersea cables and of the global fibre optic cable that links all the continents of the world. The cables were considered so important that during the 2nd World War tin miners were drafted in to hew out bomb proof chambers in the granite cliffs. The chambers can now be visited as now part of the Museum of Submarine Telegraphy.

Minack Theatre

Open air theatre created on the cliff top above Porthcurno and the setting for plays during the summer. Even the famous Greek ampitheatre's of antiquity would find it hard to match the grand backdrop of the sea and setting sun. Don't forget to take a picnic and some rugs.

St Levan's Church

Beautifully sited medieval church undoubtedly standing on a very ancient site. St Levan is thought to have landed at Porth Chapel. The great fissured stone in the churchyard was a favourite resting place of St Levan where he would sit and watch the sea. He broke the stone with his staff and legend says that the world will end when a donkey with loaded panniers can pass through the fissure. The stone crosses in the churchyard probably marked the holy enclosure before a church was ever built here. Two other Celtic crosses are found within a few hundred metres of the church marking the paths that radiate from the church. The churchyard holds some of the graves of victims of the *Khyber*, wrecked at Porth Loe in 1904.

St Levan's Well & Chapel

The holy well is attributed with magical powers and is said to be particularly effective in curing tooth and eye complaints. The well is still used for baptisms. St Levan in common with many Cornish saints lived as a hermit. The foundations of his small cell are visible on the cliff below the well.

A Stroll Around Gwennap Head

*Distance: 1 mile round trip - add 3 miles if you walk to Nanjizal to watch the seals. **Going:** Generally OK. Easy assent from the car park if you follow the road up to the old coastguard houses. The walk to Nanjizal is fairly easy but with some sharp descents and assents into river valleys at Trevean and Nanjizal. **Car Parking:** Large car park at Porthgwarra. **Refreshments:** Ice creams available at Porthgwarra in the summer.*

Coastguard Lookout

Gwennap Head is known as the fisherman's Land's End because of the turbulent currents created by the meeting of two tides. As the tide rises it pushes water into the English Channel. The water backs up, blocked by the narrowing of the Channel at the Straits of Dover. This makes the water level higher in the English Channel than in the Irish sea which is less constrained. It is between Gwennap Head and Cape Cornwall that the water levels merge leading to fast swirling currents visible from the cliffs.

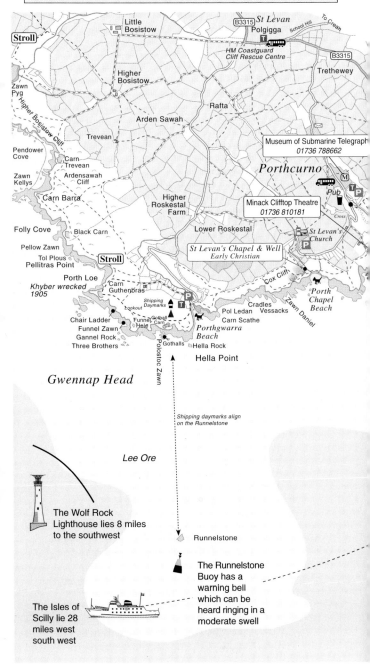

St Buryan

One can sense in St Buryan the move
from the sheltered villages of
Mousehole and Lamorna to this
exposed plateau. The church
and houses appear to have
been built to stand
foursquare against the
elements rather than
hiding away. Having
said that in the
summer the
flowers and
warmth of the
stone seem
all the more
charming.

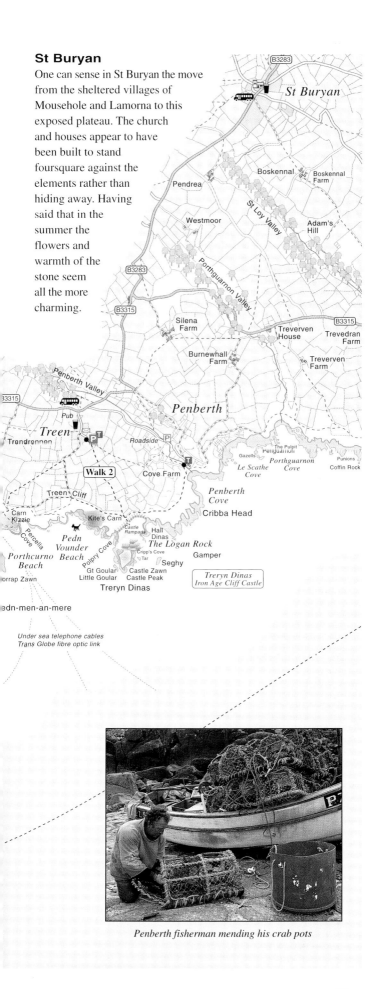

Penberth fisherman mending his crab pots

Walk 2. Treen Cliff and the Logan Rock

This wonderful cliff walk starts from Treen Village but may also start from Penberth. Look out for the gorse covered in the pink thread mats of dodder - a unusual parasitic plant. The walk takes in Treryn Dinas an Iron Age cliff castle and at Porthcurno you can take a tour of the cliff tunnels built to protect the telephone cable station. Combines many of the elements that make West Cornwall so special - the sense of ancient history the intense beauty of the beaches set against the cliffs.

Distance: 3 miles round trip (2 hours) - add 1 mile if you start at Penberth. Going: Generally easy along Treen Cliff to Porthcurno - steep climb out of Penberth on the coast path. The climb to the Logan Rock is difficult. Car Parking: Large car park at Treen. Limited roadside parking at Penberth best avoided in busy summer months. Pub/Refreshments: Pasties & ice creams available at Treen post office. The Logan Rock pub at Treen serves food. Pub & shops at Porthcurno

> *Leave Treen and follow the path seaward, along the side of the car park and over the fields. This will bring you directly to the entrance to Treryn Dinas.*

Treryn Dinas

One of the best preserved Iron Age cliff castles in Cornwall. The headland is a natural defensive site with only the landward side needing earth ramparts. The present entrance is probably the site of the original gate. The earth ramparts were probably surmounted with a wooden palisade. It is difficult to see the site as being a permanent settlement because it is so exposed with no fresh water and enclosing a relatively small area. Perhaps it would have been the Iron Age equivalent of an air raid shelter used on in times of imminent danger from raiding Norsemen.

Logan Rock

Inside the cliff castle and on top of the second large out crop of granite is a *logan* or *rocking stone*. Common throughout Cornwall on the tops of carns these stones sit on a tiny point of contact with the rock beneath. In such cases it was possible for a child to rock a block of granite weighing many tons backwards and forwards. Don't get too excited because this logan stone will not move. It was levered out of place by a Lt. Goldsmith of HMS Nimble in 1824. The locals were outraged and he was forced by the Admiralty to erect an elaborate pulley mechanism to retrieve the rock and place it back in its original position. The same apparatus was also used to replace the capstone of Lanyon Quoit.

> *As you pass out through the ramparts turn left along the footpath to Porthcurno. Soon a path crosses the coast path - turn left and down the path for Pedn-vounder Beach.*

4. Land's End & Sennen Cove

Wreck of the Bluejacket *on a clear night in 1898*

The coast around Land's End is very popular but none the worse for it, especially if you visit in the evening to watch the sun go down over the Longships and the Isles of Scilly. If you cannot avoid the crowds during the day, try walking a little further than many visitors to the **Enys Dodman** with its resident seabirds.

Nanjizal Bay

Peaceful, boulder strewn cove. Never busy and always worth exploring. The cove was full of golden sand until about 20 years ago when storms swept most of it away - an extreme example of a common process on local beaches. Stroll down to Nanjizal through Trevilley hamlet.

Land's End

Despite its fame and popularity Land's End has lost none of its attraction. The sheer grandeur of the situation is overwhelming. A visit to the Land's End Theme Park is surprisingly enjoyable. There are displays and information on the history and wildlife of this part of the coast. **Dollar Cove** is the scene of a recently rediscovered wreck, thought to contain millions of pounds worth of Spanish gold.

Sennen Cove

The most popular beach in West Cornwall with a mile of wonderful sand. The granite rocks vary tremendously in texture and colour with delightful rock pools.

Stroll between Sennen Cove & Land's End

This popular stroll along the high cliffs has great views to the Longships rocks and lighthouse and on a clear day to the Isles of Scilly. If you want to avoid the crowds come in the evening.

Distance: 2 miles round trip (2 hours). *Going: Easy.*
Car Parking: Large car parks at Sennen & Land's End. The Land's End car park is more expensive. *Bus: Regular service to St Ives along spectacular north coast road & to Penzance.*
Pub/Refreshments: Cafe & pubs in Sennen & Land's End. The Hotel at Land's End serves evening meals.

Leave Sennen Cove and head towards the old lookout at Pedn-men-du. The coast path is easy to follow from here.

Mayon Cliff Barrow

Well preserved Bronze Age burial mound right beside the coast path with clearly visible retaining kerb.

Maen Castle

Early Iron Age cliff castle with well preserved earth and stone ramparts on the north side. Small but less bleak than many similar cliff castles. A number of archaeological finds from the interior of the castle are exhibited at Penlee House Museum & Gallery in Penzance.

Land's End

*Carn Creis Barrows
(Bronze Age Burial Mound)*

Whitesand Bay

Longships Lighthouse

The present lighthouse was started
in 1870 and replaced a smaller and
unsatisfactory light commissioned
in 1794. The keepers took watch in
shifts and their families lived in the
row of houses at Land's End. The
lighthouse is now automated.

° Little Bo

Bo Cowloe

The Tribbe

Shark's Fin

Old Lookout
Pedn-mên-du
Irish Lady Rk
Carn-mên-ellas

*Mayon Cliff
Bronze Age Burial mound*

*Maen Castle
(Iron Age Cliff Castle)*

Castle Zawn

May
Cliff

Ca
Cliff

Fillis

Kettle's Bottom

Maenek

Longships Lighthouse

Carn Bras *The Longships*

Tal-y-maen

Dr Syntax's Head

The Peal

Land's End Dollar Cove
Peber

Dr Johnson's Head

Greeb Zawn

The Armed Knight

Gamper
Bay

Carn Clog
Gamper Hole

Stroll

*Land's End
Theme Park*

Carn
Greeb

Enys Dodman
Zawn Tor
Zawn Wells

Pordenack Point

Lion's Den

Carn
Enys

Carn
Cheer

Ca
Be

Zawn Trevilley
Carn
Sperm

Carn Boe

The Wolf Rock Lighthouse

One of the most exposed lighthouses
in the British Isles. Waves frequently
breaking over the top of the 35m tower
in storms. This drove one of the first, solitary
keepers mad with fear and led to the rule that
there should be at least two keepers on the
lighthouse at any one time. It is said that the rock
is called the Wolf because of the howling noise
caused by high winds as they are forced between the
walls of a cleft in the rock. The first lighthouse took
seven years to build and was finished in 1862 after all earlier
attempts were destroyed by the first winter storms. It is now
fully automated with a helicopter platform for maintenance.

*Wolf Rock Lighthouse
9 miles south west of
Land's End*

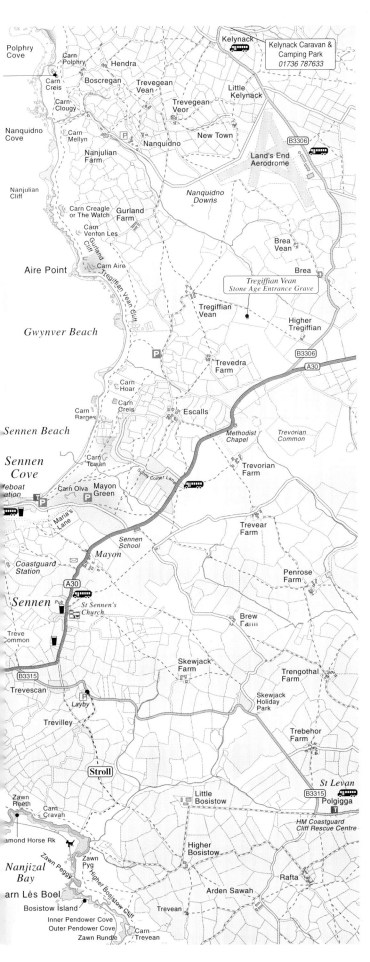

Polphry
Cove

Kelynack

Kelynack Caravan &
Camping Park
01736 787633

Carn
Polphry

Hendra

Carn
Creis

Boscregan

Trevegean
Vean

Little
Kelynack

Carn
Clougy

Trevegean
Veor

New Town

B3306

Nanquidno
Cove

Carn
Mellyn

Nanjulian
Farm

Nanquidno

Land's End
Aerodrome

Nanjulian
Cliff

*Nanquidno
Downs*

Carn Creagle
or The Watch

Gurland
Farm

Brea
Vean

Carn
Venton Les

Brea

Aire Point

Carn Aire

*Tregiffian Vean
Stone Age Entrance Grave*

Gwynver Beach

Tregiffian
Vean

Higher
Tregiffian

P

Trevedra
Farm

B3306

A30

Carn
Hoar

Carn
Creis

Escalls

Carn
Barges

*Methodist
Chapel*

*Trevorian
Common*

Sennen Beach

Carn
Towan

**Sennen
Cove**

Trevorian
Farm

Sydney Corner Lane

Lifeboat
Station

Carn Olva

Mayon
Green

P

Trevear
Farm

P

*Maria's
Lane*

*Sennen
School*

Mayon

*Coastguard
Station*

Penrose
Farm

A30

Sennen   Pub

*St Sennen's
Church*

Brew
Farm

Treve
Common

Skewjack
Farm

Trengothal
Farm

B3315

Skewjack
Holiday
Park

Trevescan

Layby

Trevilley

Trebehor
Farm

Stroll

St Levan

Little
Bosistow

B3315
Polgigga

Zawn
Reeth

Carn
Cravah

*HM Coastguard
Cliff Rescue Centre*

Diamond Horse Rk

Higher
Bosistow

Zawn Peggy

Zawn
Pyg

*Nanjizal
Bay*

Rafta

Carn Lês Boel

Higher Bosistow Cliff

Arden Sawah

Bosistow Island

Inner Pendower Cove
Outer Pendower Cove
Zawn Rundle

Trevean

Carn
Trevean

27

5. Carn Euny & the Prehistoric Landscape

Caer Bran Iron Age hillfort. Top left - open shafts and mine workings from the 18th & 19th centuries. Bottom left is a circular 'round' or defended homestead probably Iron Age.

In the last section we saw an important and early example of an Iron Age Cliff castle in **Maen Cliff Castle** near to **Sennen Cove**. In this section we cover another important Iron Age site, the excavated prehistoric village at **Carn Euny** which lies at the centre of a concentration of archaeological sites that span 5,000 years. Both Maen Cliff Castle and Carn Euny Prehistoric Village lie on an prehistoric track that was probably ancient even in the Iron Age. This track is known as the **'Old Land's End Road'** and originally linked Maen Cliff Castle and Sennen Cove to Mount's Bay via the hills of **Chapel Carn Brea**, **Caer Bran** and **Sancreed Beacon**.

The Isles of Scilly can clearly be seen from Maen Castle and Mayon Cliff and we know that in the Neolithic or New Stone Age there had to be communication between the Isles of Scilly and the Land's End Peninsula, because the Scillonian chamber tombs or entrance graves occur both here and on Scilly. In fact there is an entrance grave on Mayon Cliff just beside the cliff path. It is likely, although unproven that Sennen Cove would have been used as a harbour even in the Stone Age as it gives some degree of shelter and also has a wide sandy beach for landing boats, both important factors on this exposed and rocky coast.

Some parts of the track have been lost but most of the route on the high ground can be easily followed. Each successive hilltop is crowned by a tomb which often stands out on the skyline. This is a pattern also found on another prehistoric track - **The Tinners' Way** which runs from Cape Cornwall to St Ives (See page 32). The walk starts and finishes with panoramic views across the whole southern part of the Land's End Peninsula. Chapel Carn Brea looks west to the Isles of Scilly and is itself crowned by a large Scillonian chamber tomb. Sancreed Beacon looks east to Mount's Bay and St Michael's Mount. The star of this walk has to be Carn Euny Prehistoric Village. Here one finds not only monuments but the homes of the people that built them - you can walk into the houses that they lived in, over stone paved floors that they laid 2,000 years ago.

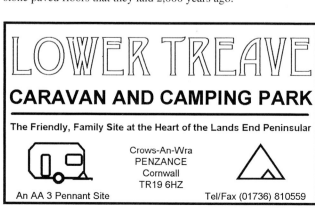
Please mention this Friendly Guide when replying to advertisements

Carn Euny Prehistoric Village

The majority of the visible remains at Carn Euny date from the Iron Age but unlike the classic courtyard settlement at Chysauster it seems to have evolved in a more organic way. The village incorporates both round houses and a variant type of courtyard house which surprisingly lacks the large round house element. What makes Carn Euny very special is the rare underground corbelled chamber and the exceptionally well preserved underground passage or *fogou*. The corbelled chamber and its entrance passage seem to have been the earliest structures - they date from about 500BC. The fogou was built later, cutting the entrance passage at right angles and with its only entrance being via the *creep passage* at the west end. The final stage was the opening up of the east end

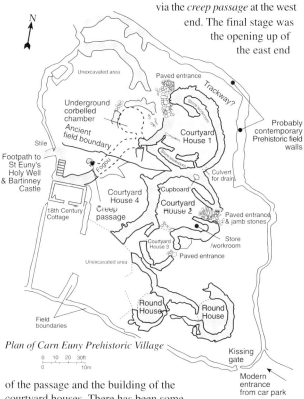

Plan of Carn Euny Prehistoric Village

of the passage and the building of the courtyard houses. There has been some speculation that the courtyard houses had some ceremonial function because they do not incorporate the usual round house in their plan. The paved entrance to Courtyard House 1 is well preserved and feels rather 'grand' and again it is suggested that this was an important ceremonial entrance to the fogou. Unfortunately, we have very little idea what function a fogou performed.

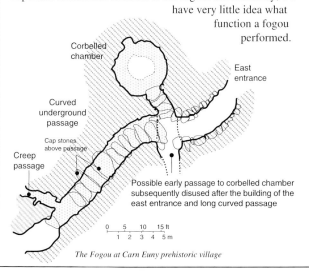

The Fogou at Carn Euny prehistoric village

Carn Euny Fogou. Looking towards the entrance to the corbelled chamber.

Walk 2. Chapel Carn Brea - Carn Euny - Caer Bran- Sancreed Beacon

Distance: *3 miles (3 hours).* ***Going:*** *Easy.*
Car Parking: *Small car parks at Chapel Carn Brea, Carn Euny and Sancreed Beacon. Limited roadside parking at Sancreed Church.* ***Bus:*** *Infrequent service from Pz to Sancreed. More frequent Land's End /Pz service - alight at Crows-an-wra.*
Refreshments/Pub: *Nearest pubs at St Buryan & Newbridge. Best to take a picnic and enjoy the views from Sancreed Beacon or take lunch in a courtyard house at Carn Euny Prehistoric Village.*

Chapel Carn Brea

The last hill in Britain with panoramic views to the south and west. A bonfire is lit on the summit on Midsummer's Eve to mark the summer solstice. Large, ruined Stone Age entrance grave on summit.

St Euny's Well

Typical tiny Celtic well. The water was supposed to have curative properties.

Carn Euny Prehistoric Village

Excavated Iron Age village and fogou. See previous page.
① *Leave Carn Euny by the footpath and stile at the west end of the fogou & follow first the track then the footpath to Caer Bran hillfort.*

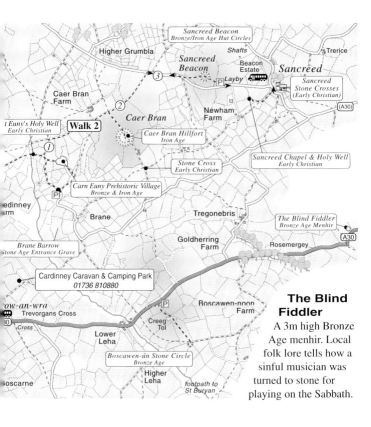

The Blind Fiddler

A 3m high Bronze Age menhir. Local folk lore tells how a sinful musician was turned to stone for playing on the Sabbath.

Caer Bran

Iron Age hillfort with large earth ramparts. Associated with Carn Euny Prehistoric Village below.

② *Return to the track, turn right and walk to the main road. Turn*
③ *right an follow the road towards Sancreed Beacon.*

Sancreed Beacon

Bronze/Iron Age hut circles just below summit. There is an information board at the site by the lay-by. The views across Mount's Bay are great.

*You can continue the walk to Sancreed Church & Holy Well -
it adds about 1 mile to the walk.*

Sancreed Church

There are two large Celtic crosses in the churchyard dating from the Dark Ages. In appearance they mimic the Bronze Age *menhirs* and are carved with Christ figures, one with intricate knotwork patterns. The church has a beautiful rood screen separating the nave from the altar. It is one of the few to have survived the Reformation and is covered in carvings. One is of a king who simultaneously looks to the past, present and future - a survival from Celtic religion.

Sancreed Chapel & Holy Well

The ruined chapel may date from the 7th or 8th centuries. The well is often 'dressed' with pieces of cloth another survival from Celtic religion.

6. The Tinners Way

As we have seen in the previous section about Carn Euny one of the special aspects of the landscape of the Land's End Peninsula is the large number and quality of the ancient monuments and villages. In ancient times these settlements were all linked by track ways. One of the most complete tracks runs from Cape Cornwall towards St Ives following the high ground above the north coast and linking many of the most impressive archaeological sites. This track is popularly known as the *Tinners Way*.

The whole walk can be done in a day by anyone who is reasonably fit but is easily split into smaller sections. Each one becoming the basis for a number of walks across the moors. The route can be walked in either direction starting from St Ives or St Just. If you are walking the whole way from St Just it is more interesting to end the walk at Zennor because you can take in Zennor Hill and Quoit and finish at Zennor Head with its great views.

Most of the track is clear so detailed directions are not necessary. You can usually get your bearings in relation to a few obvious landmarks especially the old engine house on Greenbarrow Shaft of Ding Dong Mine. The coast road has a regular bus service in the summer between St Just and St Ives and you can get off almost anywhere and make your way up onto the high ground and the track.

Section 1. Cape Cornwall to Kenidjack Carn

If you are starting the walk from this end I would suggest starting at Cape Cornwall or at St Just but if you have decided to walk westwards finish at Kenidjack Castle where there are fantastic views.

Distance: 3 miles (2 hours). *Car parking:* Cape Cornwall, Botallack, St Just & at the fork of the B3318 west of Chun Castle. *Buses:* Regular buses from Penzance & St Ives to St Just.

Going: Easy - may be overgrown in parts. *Refreshments/Pubs:* Cream Teas at Tregeseal, Pubs at Botallack & St Just (try The Star).

Cape Cornwall
See opposite.

Kenidjack Castle
The ramparts are on the north side of the headland guarding Porthledden Cove which was a safe landing beach. The view to the west is to the Isles of Scilly, Longships Lighthouse & Land's End beyond Cape Cornwall. To the north you can see the perilously positioned Crowns Engine Houses

Tregeseal Nine Maidens & Kenidjack Carn
Concentration of monuments including stone circles, small holed stones and Stone Age barrows. The carn is known locally as Hooting Carn and is widely rumoured to be haunted.

---

7. Cape Cornwall, St Just & Pendeen

Tin miners working in one of the undersea galleries of Levant Mine

This was the heart of the tin & copper mining area of West Cornwall until the closure of **Geevor Mine** in 1992. Almost every part of the cliffs and moors in this area have been mined, sometimes several times over as new technology allowed lower concentrations of metal to be recovered. In some places this has created a strange lunar landscape of spoil heaps. The ruins of mine buildings and processing floors have taken on a curious grandeur almost as if they were Grecian or Roman remains. Everywhere you look there are mine engine houses that were used for pumping, lifting and crushing. The most spectacularly sited engine houses are **The Crowns** below Botallack Counthouse.

Whilst you are in the area you must take the opportunity to go underground at **Geevor Mine Museum** and experience the sensation of the all enveloping darkness of a mine. Just along the coast from Geevor, and within walking distance is **Levant Mine** where the National Trust and Trevithick Trust have preserved the last working mine steam engine in the county.

St Just

St Just is the capital of the mining district. During the boom mining years in the first half of the 19th century the place was pretty wild with heavy drinking, obstreperous miners. It took John Wesley and his fire and brimstone preaching to subdue them. There was something in the hellfire which appealed to the Cornish spirit. The importance of Methodism is symbolised by the grand view leading up to the Methodist chapel. An interesting survival is the grassy amphitheatre the Plen-an-Gwary where medieval miracle plays were performed.

Cape Cornwall

For many years until the Ordnance Survey proved otherwise it was thought that Cape Cornwall was the most westerly point in Britain hence its status as a cape - separating the English and Bristol Channels. Small boats fish from Priest's Cove on the south side and every at the Cape Games a swimming race is held from The Brisons.

Wheal Edward & West Wheal Owles

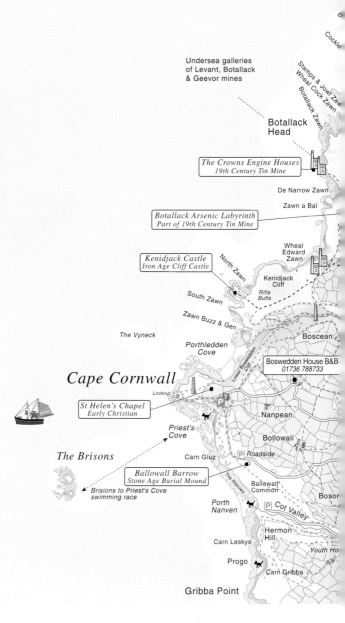

Cockle

Undersea galleries
of Levant, Botallack
& Geevor mines

Stamps & Jowl Zaw
Wheal Cock Zawn

Botallack Zawn

**Botallack
Head**

The Crowns Engine Houses
19th Century Tin Mine

De Narrow Zawn

Zawn a Bal

Botallack Arsenic Labyrinth
Part of 19th Century Tin Mine

Wheal
Edward
Zawn

Kenidjack Castle
Iron Age Cliff Castle

North Zawn

Kenidjack
Cliff

Rifle
Butts

South Zawn

Zawn Buzz & Gen

The Vyneck

Porthledden
Cove

Boscean

Lower Boswedden Cliff

Boswedden House B&B
01736 788733

Cape Cornwall

Lookout

St Helen's Chapel
Early Christian

Nanpean

Priest's
Cove

Bollowall

The Brisons

Carn Gluz

Roadside

Ballowall Barrow
Stone Age Burial Mound

The Ribows

Ballowall
Common

Bosor

*Brisions to Priest's Cove
swimming race*

Porth
Nanven

Cot Valley

Hermon
Hill

Carn Leskys

Youth Ho

Progo

Carn Gribba

Gribba Point

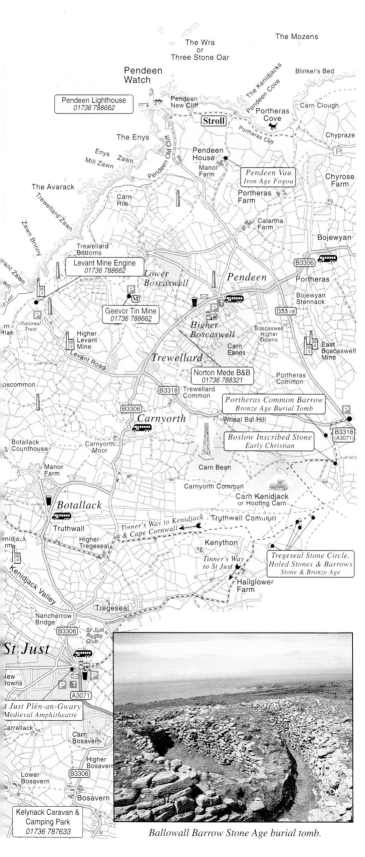

The Mozens

The Wra
or
Three Stone Oar

Pendeen
Watch

The Kenidjacks

Pendeen Cove

Blinker's Bed

Pendeen Lighthouse
01736 788662

Pendeen
New Cliff

Portheras
Cove

Carn Clough

Stroll

Portheras Cliff

Chypraze

The Enys

The Avarack

Enys
Mill Zawn

Enys
Zawn

Pendeen Old Cliff

Pendeen
House

Manor
Farm

Pendeen Vau
Iron Age Fogou

Chyrose
Farm

Trewellard Zawn

Zawn Brinny

Carn
Rôs

Portheras
Farm

Calartha
Farm

Bojewyan

ant Zawn

National
Trust

Trewellard
Bottoms

Levant Mine Engine
01736 788662

Lower
Boscaswell

Pendeen

Portheras

B3306

Zawn

Geevor Tin Mine
01736 788662

Higher
Boscaswell

Boscaswell
Higher
Downs

Bojewyan
Stennack

B3318

Higher
Levant
Mine

Levant Road

Trewellard

Carn
Eanes

East
Boscaswell
Mine

oscommon

Carnyorth

Norton Mede B&B
01736 788321

B3318

Trewellard
Common

Portheras
Common

B3306

Wheal Bal Hill

Portheras Common Barrow
Bronze Age Burial Tomb

B3318
(A3071)

Botallack
Counthouse

Carnyorth
Moor

Boslow Inscribed Stone
Early Christian

Manor
Farm

Carn Bean

Carnyorth Common

Botallack

Carn Kenidjack
or Hooting Carn

nidjack
rm

Truthwall

Higher
Tregeseal

Tinner's Way to Kenidjack
& Cape Cornwall

Truthwall Common

Kenython

Kenidjack Valley

Tinner's Way
to St Just

Tregeseal Stone Circle,
Holed Stones & Barrows
Stone & Bronze Age

Hailglower
Farm

Tregeseal

Nancherrow
Bridge

B3306

St Just
Rugby
Club

St Just

New
Downs

A3071

St Just Plên-an-Gwary
Medieval Amphitheatre

Carrallack

Carn
Bosavern

Higher
Bosavern

Lower
Bosavern

B3306

Bosavern

Kelynack Caravan &
Camping Park
01736 787633

Ballowall Barrow Stone Age burial tomb.

A Brief History of Mining Around St just

Tin and copper ore in West Cornwall occur in exceptionally concentrated veins or *lodes*. The ore is sometimes as much as 10% pure metal as opposed to the less than 1% found in alluvial deposits elsewhere in the world. It is this high concentration of metal that has made it economic to mine ore in the hard rock and under the difficult conditions found in West Cornwall. The lodes tend to occur as near vertical sheets within the surrounding rock, often only one or two feet wide and generally running in a north west-south east alignment. Where the lodes outcrop on the cliffs the sea exploits the line of weakness represented by the join of the lode to the rock, to erode deep gullies locally known as *zawns*. Many of the early lodes must have been discovered by following the line of the zawns or by locating the green copper verdigris that weeps from the rock when a copper load is exposed to the atmosphere.

The mineral lodes are also being constantly eroded by the elements from above so that the heavy tin ore is found in naturally graded concentrations within the beds of streams in the area. It was probably this easily accessible *stream tin* that was first utilised by the Bronze Age people to make farming implements and weapons - bronze is an alloy of tin and copper. Bronze Age swords and spears dating back 3,000 years can be seen at **Penlee House Museum** in Penzance and at the **Royal Cornwall Museum** in Truro. There is some evidence to suggest that copper and tin ingots were being exported from **St Michael's Mount** to the Mediterranean 2,000 years ago. This must have been a lucrative trade perhaps helping to finance the building the bijoux Iron Age courtyard houses at **Chysauster**.

As the sources of stream tin became exhausted in the first few centuries after AD1000, miners started to dig out the lodes from the solid rock by enlarging the natural zawns and also working from above to form deep gullies or *coffins* . At this time there where two natural limits on the development of tin and copper production. Firstly, the ore and the surrounding rock was simply so hard that contemporary tools had trouble making any headway. Secondly, as the workings reached the water table they soon became flooded. The problem of flooding was solved to some extent by driving tunnels or *adits* in from the cliff base allowing water to flow out to the sea and thereby lowering the water table. It was not until the early 19th century that the new technology of steam driven pumps allowed the mines to be worked below the water table for the first time - the pumps drawing water up to the level of the adit to be drained away. Coupled with the timely invention of dynamite the mines rapidly expanded, reaching depths of over 1,000 feet 'below adit' and extending outwards below the sea. At **Levant Mine** the undersea galleries were worked to within a few feet of the sea bed and it is said that during severe storms the rumble of boulders being throw along the sea bed could clearly be heard in the mine galleries below.

The miners worked on a self employed basis, bidding against

Please mention this Friendly Guide when replying to advertisements

The Crowns engine houses of Botallack Mine about 1860

one another to work a set lode for the owner and taking a proportion of the profit. The working conditions in the cramped and narrow lodes were hard. Constant dampness combined with intense heat given off by the surrounding rocks. The average life expectancy of a miner was less than 40 years. The competitive nature of the bidding for lodes and the independence of spirit of the miners themselves, worked against the organisation of the miners into unions that might have improved conditions.

Fortunes were made as production in the mines peaked in the middle of the 19th century. Foremost in this area where the Bolitho family who own **Trengwainton House** near Penzance and are still large landowners. At one time they owned a bank, a smelting works as well as a number of mines. The good times could not last forever and the tin price collapsed in the 1880's as new, cheaper, overseas alluvial tin swamped the market and many miners were forced to emigrate. They found work in the diamond and gold mines of Canada, Mexico, South Africa and Australia. To this day the links are kept up with many descendants visiting the land of their great grandfathers.

Geevor was the last mine in West Cornwall, it finally closed in 1992 ending 3,000 years of continuous mining industry. What remains of the mines is mostly on the surface - the engine houses such as **The Crowns** near **Botallack** perched on the edge of the cliff and the spoil dumps which are now slowly being reclaimed by plants and animals to create a new habitat. Another less visible legacy are the hundreds of shafts and miles of underground galleries. The shafts litter the landscape and have a wonderful presence and air of mystery. They seem to be the physical embodiment of the Celtic belief in the underworld and it is easy to see why mining has an almost symbolic importance to the Cornish.

Further Reading:
St Just - An Archaeological Survey of the Mining District - Vol. 1 & 2. Cornwall Archeological Unit. *Very detailed analysis of the mining sites.*

8. Morvah, Carn Galva to Zennor

In winter this is the most deserted and bleak part of the Land's End Peninsula. A thin strip of fields is sandwiched between the sea and the moors. Gales blast in from the Atlantic and huge waves break over offshore reefs and rocks. One gets the feeling that even in the summer the tiny farming villages such as **Morvah** and **Zennor** sit anchored ready to brace themselves against a sudden storm. The solid, wind blown buildings contrast wonderfully against the sudden flowering of delicate wild plants in May and June. In the autumn the hillsides turn a stunning auburn colour as the bracken starts to die back. The best walks are on the high ground which starts at **Watch Croft** - the highest part of the Land's End Peninsula and continues east to **Carn Galva** and **Zennor Hill** - all have fine views. The best coastal walks are from the Gurnard's Head Hotel (pub) to the **Gurnard's Head** and the short stroll to **Long Carn** from the car park below **Watch Croft** where you can sit perched high above the sea.

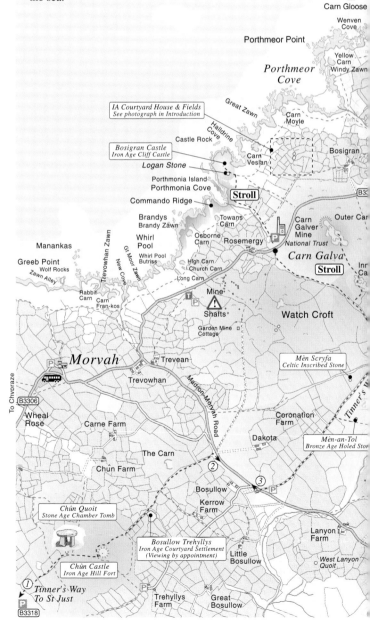

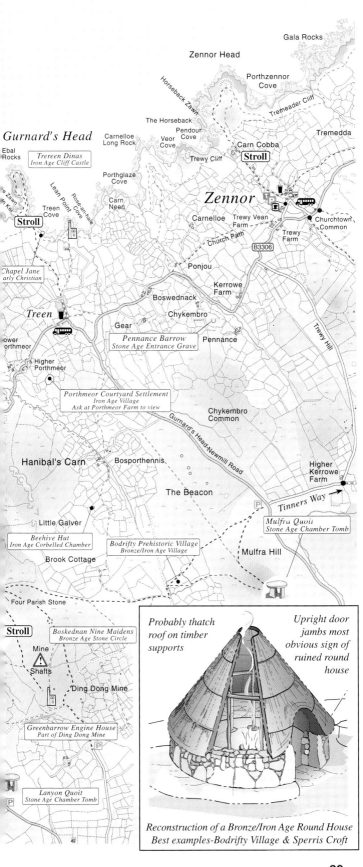

Gala Rocks

Zennor Head

Porthzennor Cove

Tremeader Cliff

Horseback Zawn

The Horseback

Pendour Cove

Tremedda

Gurnard's Head

Carnelloe Long Rock

Veor Cove

Carn Cobba

Stroll

Ebal Rocks

Trereen Dinas
Iron Age Cliff Castle

Trewy Cliff

Porthglaze Cove

Rose-an-hale Cove

Carn Neen

Zennor

Churchtown

Churchtown Common

Lean Point

Treen Cove

Stroll

Carnelloe

Trewy Vean Farm

Trewy Farm

Church Path

B3306

Ponjou

Chapel Jane
Early Christian

Kerrowe Farm

Boswednack

Chykembro

Treen

Gear

Pennance Barrow
Stone Age Entrance Grave

Pennance

Lower Porthmeor

Higher Porthmeor

Porthmeor Courtyard Settlement
Iron Age Village
Ask at Porthmeor Farm to view

Trewy Hill

Chykembro Common

Gurnard's Head/Newmill Road

Hanibal's Carn

Bosporthennis

The Beacon

Higher Kerrowe Farm

Tinners Way

Little Galver

Beehive Hut
Iron Age Corbelled Chamber

Mulfra Quoit
Stone Age Chamber Tomb

Bodrifty Prehistoric Village
Bronze/Iron Age Village

Mulfra Hill

Brook Cottage

Four Parish Stone

Stroll

Boskednan Nine Maidens
Bronze Age Stone Circle

Mine Shafts

Ding Dong Mine

Greenbarrow Engine House
Part of Ding Dong Mine

Lanyon Quoit
Stone Age Chamber Tomb

Probably thatch roof on timber supports

Upright door jambs most obvious sign of ruined round house

Reconstruction of a Bronze/Iron Age Round House
Best examples-Bodrifty Village & Sperris Croft

The Tinner's Way - 2 Chun Castle to Mulfra

Distance: $4^{1}/_{2}$ *miles ($2^{1}/_{2}$ hours).* **Going:** *Easy.*

Car Parking: *Car parks at the fork of the B3318 west of Chûn Hill and some vergeside parking on the Gurnard's Head Road opposite the turning towards Higher Kerrowe Farm.*

Pub/Refreshments: *Nothing en route - best to bring a picnic and stop at Bodrifty Prehistoric Village. Nearest pubs - Gurnard's Head Hotel at Treen & the Tinner's Arms at Zennor.*

From the car park follow the path up Chûn Hill towards Chûn Quoit which is clearly visible on the skyline.

Chûn Quoit

The first and best preserved in a string of Stone Age chamber tombs on the sides of hills above the north coast. This one is almost undamaged - only missing the covering mound of earth & stones.

Chûn Castle

Unusually for West Cornwall this Iron Age hill fort has stone ramparts rather than the more usual earth banks. The castle has been robbed of much stone but even its present state it is quite imposing. Constructed of three concentric rings of ramparts originally standing up to 3 metres high.

Follow the path down the hill, past Bosullow Trehyllys Settlement.

Bosullow Trehyllys Courtyard Settlement

Iron Age courtyard settlement. Sits under the protective umbrella of Chûn Castle with which it is contemporary. If you want to visit the site you will need to make an appointment. There is a contact number on the wooden entrance gate to the site.

Follow the path to the main road. Turn right, continue for 500m. Turn left off the road & follow the sign post to the Men-an-Tol.

Mên-an-Tol

Famous and enigmatic Bronze Age holed stone. Large enough for a child to crawl through and part of an alignment of stones. Folk lore attributes healing properties to the stone. It is said to be able to cure children of rickets if they crawl through the stone nine times towards the setting sun. Photograph page 47.

Continue on the main path to the Four Parish Stone which marks the boundaries of Zennor, Madron, Gulval and Morvah parishes. You can make a detour to Carn Galva by turning left. Carn Galva has views over the prehistoric field boundaries around Bosigran.

Boskednan Nine Maidens Stone Circle

Small, ruined BA stone circle that sits on a saddle of ground between two natural basins in the landscape. In common with many stone circles its siting seems intended to observe and receive the landscape rather than to dominate it.

Bodrifty Prehistoric Village

Settlement of hut circles or round houses with a low defensive earthwork. Some of the hut circles may date from the late Bronze Age and it was certainly in occupation during the Iron Age. The site makes an interesting contrast with the settlements at Carn Euny and Chysauster whose more sophisticated courtyard houses never seem to have gained the popularity and widespread use of the simple round house plan. Invite yourself into one of the houses and take lunch in the exact spot and the way the original inhabitants would have done 2,000 years ago. More information on display boards around the site.

Mulfra Quoit

This section ends as it began at Chûn Quoit with panoramic views this time looking over Mount's Bay and the Channel.

9. Zennor to St Ives

The Bessemer City *wrecked at Brea Cove 1941*

This final part of the coastline is centred around the little hamlet of Zennor. For its small size it has a range of facilities that would the envy of many larger villages. Of the six houses one is lovely little museum in the old mill, one a cafe in the old chapel, and one is a famous pub. Half the village is dedicated to the pleasure - a proportion that would make Las Vagas green with envy.

Zennor makes a perfect starting and finishing point to exploring this part of the coast. A stroll down the valley to Zennor Head takes only 15 minutes and is best done in the evening as the sun sets over the sea then waiting until twilight to return to the pub. Rising above Zennor is Churchtown Common and Zennor Hill with its views over the coastal shelf and along the coast. Again best to visit in the evening perhaps taking a picnic to the top of Zennor Hill. As a relief from the windswept moors I have also included a longer walk to River Cove from Wicca Farm which would take a pleasant afternoon to complete with lunch above Economy Cove.

A Stroll up Zennor Hill to Zennor Quoit

Zennor Hill suffered a bad moorland fire in 1997 - one of the worst in living memory. The up side of this is that the fire cleared away a lot of normally impenetrable gorse and other vegetation so that the hut circles on Sperris Croft are particularly clear.

Distance: 2 miles round trip (2 hours). **Going:** *A number of paths lead up to Zennor Hill & Sperris Croft. The quickest way up is by the path that leaves the main road just up from the red telephone box. This is quite a scramble. Alternatively you can walk along the track towards Foage Farm and turn up the National Trust path. The easiest path to the top leaves on the other side of the hill from Zennor at Eagle's Nest and climbs slowly up to Sperris Croft and I think almost everyone will find no problem.*

Car Parking: In Zennor. If you are taking the easy path from Eagle's Nest there is limited roadside parking in tiny lay-bys on the main road. **Pub/Refreshments:** *Tea & cakes in the old chapel; beer in the Tinner's Arms both in Zennor village.*

Zennor Quoit

Zennor Quoit dates from the late Stone Age and is unusual in having two flanking upright slabs of granite that form a consciously monumental 'entrance' to the tomb. Therefore it is possible that the whole tomb was never enclosed in mound of stone and earth and may have been left 'open' for use as a family or tribal vault. Another very ruinous chamber tomb lies 400m north east of Zennor Quoit but is almost unrecognisable as such having been robbed of stones for the nearby mine

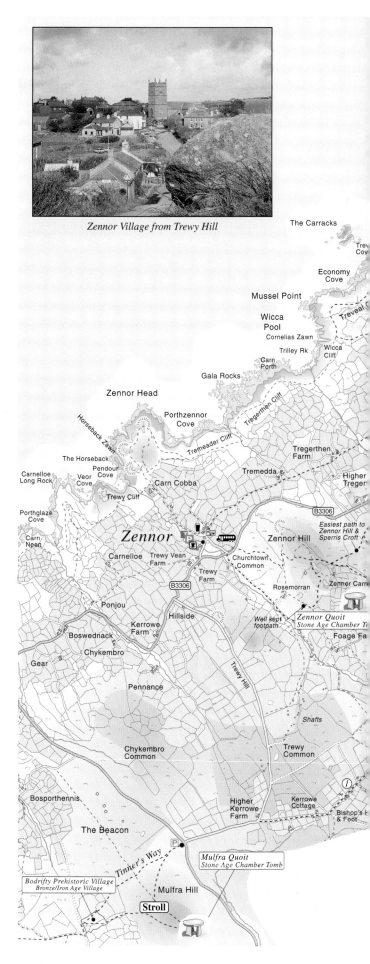

Zennor Village from Trewy Hill

River Cove

Zawn Bros

Carn Naun Point

Bowling Cove

Brea Cove

Seven Years Cove

Polgassick Rock

Polgassick Cove

Pen Enys Point

Deep Enys

Zawn Quoits

Hor Point

Trevalgan Cliff

Trowan Cliff

Carn Naun

Towednack Quae Head

Trevega Cliff

alk 4

eal Farm

Trevail Mill

Trevega Wartha

Trevega

Boscubben

Trendrine Farm

B3306

Trevalgan Farm

Trevalgan Hill

Trowan Farm

Folly Farm

B3306

P

Rosewall Hill

ca m

F

nal

Sperris Croft
Alignment of Bronze/Iron
Age Hut Circles

P

Trendrine Hill

Lower Bussow

Higher Bussow

Remains of Sperris Tin Mine

Sperris Croft

Shafts

Beagletodn Downs

Towednack

Beagletodn

Breja

Chytodden

Amalveor Downs

Water Tanks

Amalveor

*Tinner's Way
to St Ives* ➔

ner's to nor

②

The Mermaid of Zennor.
One of a number of beautifully
carved bench ends in Zennor
Church. The mermaid is said to
have enticed a local man to his
death in Pendour Cove.

Walk 4. River Cove & Wicca Pool

This walk follows one of the few sheltered and wooded valleys on the north coast. The first part from Wicca Farm to Treveal Farm follows a road sandwiched between Cornish hedges are at their full blossoming best in May & June. Seals arc often to be seen basking on the Carracks.

Distance: 3 mile round trip -2 hours.
Going: The path from Wicca Farm to River Cove is fairly easy going. Once on the coast path things become more strenuous as the path falls towards Economy Cove and then rises sharply above Wicca Pool. Car Parking: Small National Trust car park at Wicca Farm. Pub/Refreshments: Tea, cakes & beer in Zennor. Take a pasty and drinks to eat at Mussel Point.

From the National Trust car park at Wicca Farm return along the lane towards Boscubben. Turn down the tarmac road to Treveal Farm. At Treveal Farm follow the National Trust signs to Trevail Mill & River Cove.

River Cove

This is one of the few valleys on this coast that offers any shelter against the westerly storms that hit the coast in the autumn and winter. The tree cover makes this valley an important breeding habitat for birds.

The path keeps to the west side of the valley and eventually meets with the coast path.

Bowling Cove

A tiny beach from which to paddle. I have heard that people swimming from here have shared the sea with inquisitive seals who love to bask on the Carracks.

Follow the path towards Wicca Pool.

Mussel Point

Good place to stop and eat your picnic under the buttresses of Treveal Cliff.

Wicca Pool

Wicca Pool has a natural calm and beauty.

Turn inland above Cornelias Zawn to return to Treveal Farm.

The Tinner's Way - Section 3. Mulfra to Zennor & St Ives

Distance: $2^1/_2$ miles (4km) to Zennor, 5 miles (8km) to St Ives. 2 hours to Zennor, 4 hours to St Ives.
Going: No problems.
Car Parking: Vergeside parking for 3 cars opposite the turning to Zennor on the Gurnard's Head/Newmill road. Also at Towednack Church & Rosewall Hill.
Pub/Refreshments: Tinners Arms & Old Chapel cafe at Zennor village.

From Mulfra Hill cross the Newmill-Gurnard's Head Road and follow the Zennor turning to Higher Kerrowe Farm. Leave the public road and follow the track towards Amalveor Downs.

The Bishops Head & Foot

The stone here indicates the meeting point of the parishes of Gulval, Towednack and Zennor.

Follow the main track to the left past the houses and fields to the moorland. The path splits here, keep left to go to Zennor Quoit and Zennor Village. Keep right and down the hill to reach Towednack and St Ives.

10. St Ives & Trencrom Hill

Stacking pilchards in a St Ives pilchard palace

St Ives was originally called Porth Ia, after the Irish saint who landed here at sometime between the 5th and 7th centuries. She is especially revered as a protector of fishermen and in fact the old stories tell how she sailed from Ireland on a leaf.

In common with many coastal towns in Cornwall, St Ives was built on the success of the fishing industry in the nineteenth century. Many of the attractive courtyards are former pilchard palaces where fish were salted and pressed. Many small boats still work out of the harbour on the inshore reefs.

The town has a truly fantastic quality of light. This is thought to be caused by sunlight reflecting off and between the surrounding sand, sea and clouds. It was this quality of light and the picturesque appearance of the town that first attracted artists to St Ives. The town takes a special place in the history of British art in the twentieth century. Just before the Second World War a group of artists gathered here including Roger Hilton, Ben Nicholson, Christopher Wood and sculptor Barbara Hepworth. They were joined for a short period by the hugely influential Jewish artist, Naum Gabo.

In contrast to the internationally famous Gabo, the other major influence on the St Ives artists was a retired local fisherman called Alfred Wallis. Wallis had no formal artistic education and did not even start painting until late in his life. Ben Nicholson and Christopher Wood happened upon him in 1928 and brought him to the attention of the British art world. It was the naive painting style of Alfred Wallis that helped to push Wood and Nicholson towards a more abstract approach in their own work. This was something they later developed in Paris whilst working with Mondrian.

It was to show the work of these artists that the Tate Gallery opened the St Ives Tate. It is best to avoid the town centre in the summer as it can become very crowded. The Tate gallery is open late and the best time to visit is in the early evening.

St Ives at Dusk

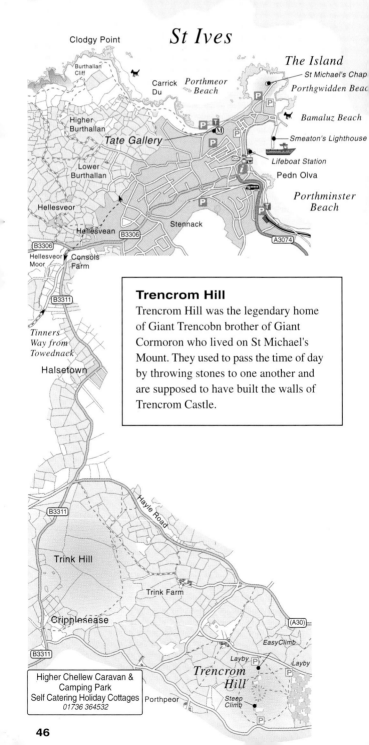

St Ives

Clodgy Point

Burthallan Cliff

Carrick Du   *Porthmeor Beach*

The Island

St Michael's Chap

Porthgwidden Beac

Higher Burthallan

Tate Gallery

Bamaluz Beach

Smeaton's Lighthouse

Lifeboat Station

Lower Burthallan

Pedn Olva

Hellesveor

Porthminster Beach

Hellesvean   B3306

Stennack

B3306

A3074

Hellesveor Moor   Consols Farm

Trencrom Hill

Trencrom Hill was the legendary home of Giant Trencobn brother of Giant Cormoron who lived on St Michael's Mount. They used to pass the time of day by throwing stones to one another and are supposed to have built the walls of Trencrom Castle.

B3311

Tinners Way from Towednack

Halsetown

B3311

Hayle Road

Trink Hill

Trink Farm

Cripplesease

A30

EasyClimb

Layby

Layby

B3311

Trencrom Hill

Higher Chellew Caravan & Camping Park
Self Catering Holiday Cottages
01736 364532

Porthpeor

Steep Climb

Gazetteer of the major archaeological sites

The Men-an-tol
Bronze Age holed stone

This list only represents the best and most accessible sites. The sites shown in **bold** are easily accessible all year around to the public. The sites in *italics* become lost in tall bracken during the summer months or are on private land and are therefore difficult to visit. Sites shown * are on the route of the Tinners Way (see page 32).

Neolithic/New Stone Age (4000-2500BC)

Ballowall Barrow, Carn Gluze
Lost for a number of years under the spoil heaps of a tin mine. A barrow of unique form.

Brane Barrow
Small and perfectly formed *entrance grave* within site of Carn Euny Prehistoric Village. Still has an intact kerb of retaining stones and roofed passage.

Tregiffian Barrow
Scillonian chamber tomb adjacent to the Merry Maidens stone circle.

Lanyon Quoit
Most famous of the Land's End chamber tombs or *quoits* and now in the care of the National Trust. Midway between Madron & Morvah (see page 39).

*Mulfra Quoit
Magnificently sited quoit overlooking Mount's Bay. Numerous footpaths to other local sites such as Bodrifty Prehistoric Village (see pages 39/42).

*Chûn Quoit
On the St Just side of Chuˆn Hill and below the later Iron Age hillfort. Parking just off the B3318 as it forks to Pendeen and Trewellard. Also within reach of Kenidjack Carn (see pages 35/38).

Bronze Age (2500-600BC)

*Mên-an-tol
Holed stone with healing properties (see page 38 & above).

Boscawen-ûn Stone Circle
Best stone circle in West Cornwall. Park at the small lay-by on A30 - look for the wooden kissing gate in the hedge (see page 31).

The Merry Maidens & the Pipers of Boleigh
Famous stone circle and associated menhirs. Also next to Stone Age entrance grave of Tregiffian Barrow (see page 18).

*Bodrifty Prehistoric Village
Excavated village of late Bronze Age/early Iron Age round houses (see page 39).

*Sperris Croft
Alignment of round houses near to Zennor Quoit (see page 43).

Iron Age/Romano-British *(600BC-400AD)*

Trencrom Hillfort

Quite a steep climb to the summit from the National Trust car park but great views up the coast to North Cornwall and south to St Michael's Mount. Original entrance to fort marked by upright stone jambs on east side. Defensive walls clearly visible on south & west sides. May have been in use in the Stone Age (see page 46).

Chysauster Prehistoric Village

Classic, excavated Iron Age village of national importance. Consists of nine courtyard houses and ruined fogou. Details of life 2,000 years ago with intact drains and thresholds. Re-enactment of Celtic life in the summer. Entrance fee and guidebook available. 1 mile north west of Newmill on Gulval-Gurnard's Head road from Penzance (see photo in Introduction).

Carn Euny Prehistoric Village & fogou

Small excavated Iron Age settlement with fabulous fogou. Consists of a number of courtyard and round houses. The children love to run in and out of the houses. Makes an excellent base to explore numerous local antiquities such as Caer Bran hillfort (see page 31).

*Bosullow Trehyllys

Overgrown courtyard house settlement adjacent to the Tinners Way and in the protective shadow of Chûn Castle. On private land the farmer will be happy to show you around. The telephone contact number is on a wooden gate at the site. There is a small entrance fee which goes to charity (see page 38).

*Chûn Castle

The best hillfort in the Land's End Peninsular. Stands above the late Stone Age Chûn Quoit and the Iron Age courtyard settlement at Bosullow Trehyllys. Parking just off the B3318 as it forks to Pendeen and Trewellard (see pages 35/38).

Dark Ages/Early Christian *(AD400-1000)*

Madron Holy Well & Chapel

Ancient Christian well still decorated with pieces of colourful rag and cloth in an almost pagan fashion. The remains of an early Medieval Christian chapel lie 75 metres further on. The chapel still has stone benches and an altar stone. A small stream runs through the building and collects in a reservoir. Baptisms are occasionally carried out here. Still revered by locals. Sign posted as *Boswarthen Chapel* off the Madron to Morvah road.

Mining Sites

The Crowns

Perched on the cliffs below Botallack Mine in the heart of the St Just mining district. Park at Botallack Counthouse above the large arsenic labyrinth.

Levant Engine House & Geevor Mine Museum

See under *What to do* on page 12.

Kenidjack Valley

Numerous mining structures in this valley leading down to Porthledden see part 7.